ENDLESS DREAMS

Angel Alexander StarWay

iUniverse, Inc.
New York   Bloomington

Endless Dreams

iUniverse books may be ordered through booksellers or by contacting:

iUniverse
1663 Liberty Drive
Bloomington, IN 47403
www.iuniverse.com
1-800-Authors (1-800-288-4677)

Because of the dynamic nature of the Internet, any Web addresses or
links contained in this book may have changed since publication and
may no longer be valid. The views expressed in this work are solely those
of the author and do not necessarily reflect the views of the publisher,
and the publisher hereby disclaims any responsibility for them.

ISBN: 978-1-4502-7433-3 (pbk)
ISBN: 978-1-4502-7432-6 (ebk)

Library of Congress Control Number: 2010917030

Printed in the United States of America

iUniverse rev. date: 11/8/2010

What truly matters

Lose all including self

To find what truly matters.

Most will never know

What is gained by losing all.

Few pass perilous trails

To find what always was.

<u>Loneliness</u>

Overwhelming sadness and loneliness

Is being in a crowded room

and knowing there's no one outside either.

To know

I miss your embrace,

The touch of your lips,

and eyes that hypnotize.

I'm so lucky to know your love.

My love

My love shines brighter

than all the suns in the universe.

My heart mourns for your love,

deeper than the darkest, coldest region of space,

creating a void without you.

Our love

Our love shall exist

As the tears we have wept and

the breaths we have taken

in sadness or happiness

Shall one day intermingle for all eternity.

Our love is and always will be.

Rain

Tears fall from the sky,

Intermingled tears from fallen lovers in the past,

Intermingled tears forever falling,

Meant to remind us not to fall.

<u>Forever joined</u>

No matter that distance separates.

Hearts that beat as one with truth

Are forever joined even

after all things come to pass.

I LOVE YOU

Near me

How I miss your strong embrace,

the softness of your smiling lips,

your hypnotic eyes

that answer my questions.

The warmth of your body

That keeps me coming back on cold needy nights.

It's torture to my senses

Even though

you're sleeping next to me,

I miss you.

Miss you

Tears, hugs, and kisses.

I hate not having you near.

I miss you.

How much do you love me?

I love you more than all the bubbles ever created in all the
oceans in the universe.

//////

Longer than all the oceans that exist and are yet to come,

Creating waves upon waves,

the endless waves that have been and will be,

Forever reminding you,

I LOVE YOU

Do you really love me?

You fear a broken heart

Glue, tape, staples,

even time,

few ways to fix,

Many ways to break.

Careless action, whispered, yelled thoughts.

How I fear breaking something fragile.

I do love you.

<u>Remembered</u>

Ideas without action are thoughts in the wind!

+

As in birth and death.

Only in death is a person's actions remembered.

In death how will you be remembered?

///

Certain actions define the memory.

<u>Violeta</u>

Many flowers and yet

only one Violeta.

//////////////////

A beloved flower

I have grown to love.

The one and only.

The one who captured my heart.

Are you happy with me?

Been soaring since I met you, and I haven't landed.

Once in a while I've hit my head on the stars and seen the moons.

/////////////////////

You're worth the eternal journey of time.

Why do you love me so?

I am, that is my answer.

My love is and will be yours.

So be it!

Do you love me?

You ask?

Mere words can never justify!

The mystics of love may never be explained.

Show and action are my reply!

How much do you miss me?

I miss you within

Like the calm waters

miss the sun's

life-giving warmth and light.

Do you miss me?

I hunger for thy lips

of savory wine

with unsatisfying craving ravines hunger within.

Kisses upon kisses; then shall I have peace.

/////////////

I miss you

like the open sky

would miss the countless stars and full moon

that light up the darkest night.

Your presence enlightens my life.

Measurement of love

Why must eternity's time be so short?

I have nothing to measure my love for you.

//////

Eternity's shortness is no measurement for infinite love.

<u>Trust in me</u>

Attainable heaven's destined distant stars.

Soar with me, share witness sights unseen.

Will you fly with me?

Soaring dream

Distance separates,

yet I dream

of soaring lonely nights,

distant skies,

chilled winds,

to your wanting, waiting embrace,

so we may share

the blissful heat,

generated by our entanglement.

Darkest night Version I

Without fear!

I love you more than the

loneliest, longest, coldest, darkest night in space,

with the knowledge that you

will save me

with hours of time-defying illuminating

body warmth.

Darkest night Version II

Without fear!

I love you more than the

loneliest, longest, coldest, darkest night in space,

with the knowledge that hours of time-defying illuminating

body warmth shall save me.

Rhythm

You're the found rhythm in my heart.

Without you, it would have been so easy,

to have let go of life's rhythm,

long ago.

Together we are the rhythm.

I Love You

Understanding

Not understanding within

Is being without.

Understanding this

is understanding the calm,

if not to seek to understand.

<u>True joy</u>

Having acknowledged

a second of true joyous happiness

is acknowledgment beyond eternity.

Self

The world is perceived through

understanding and awareness.

<u>Mystic beauty</u>

Abused toxins destroy our senses

to judge witness

on the true mystic beauty of our world.

Destiny

Paths never crossed,

Destined to never know.

Friend or Foe!

Crossed paths, forever changed

by others' destiny.

<u>Cautious remembrance</u>

Birth never a choice

Left behind,

Youthful forgotten, remembered years,

Asked to forgive.

Cautious painful remembrance.

Oh, Forgetful years.

Now you ask

Forgiveness

Never was my choice.

Left behind so young,

Years pass.

Now you ask.

Where were you when I asked?

Sanctuary

You seek sanctuary.

Your body shivers.

You seek the key.

My body warmth … is the key.

Let the softness … of my lips

take your sadness away,

As I kiss … your tears away,

My eyes … my heart … shall answer.

But you must be willing to listen,

To trust me when I say, "It'll be okay."

Torture

Please! No more!

Out loud brings more.

No strength for tears.

Barely … strength to live

Prayer and hope

are all I've got.

Freedom comes in different forms

Even though

I'm held against my will.

Another day of laughter

People laughing,

Pain,

More laughing,

More pain,

Hit after hit,

Why?

How?

The cruelty.

I could have been a friend or a

lost family member they never had.

We could have laughed together

in other ways.

Day after day,

I wait for the laughter.

Nowhere to run.

Body shakes.

Somehow I find the strength.

Another day of laughter.

Your energy

Masses called out for a solution.

A need for a pollution-free global energy.

Salvation comes

with the intense energetic hotness of your body,

powering global cities

With your walk and smile.

<u>Fools</u>

Painful tears,

meaningless life.

Fools say, "Time will heal."

Time passes, still I feel.

Destined

Thinkless knowing, envious, interfering fools,

Delighted in giving, doubt and sorrow.

To two hearts that beat as one,

Oblivious to heaven's predicted, sealed, destined born mates.

<u>War</u>

When man's fearful, lustful, cruel, hateful greed speaks,

Listen and understand man's demons.

And you shall be victorious.

Listen only, and you shall perish.

Sadness

The joy of a person's cruelty

may ruin another reality.

Sad, suffering tears are

Because of someone's fear.

Stomp on a puddle,

Someone muddled.

Stomp on a stream,

Stepped on a dream.

Strategy

I know what is to be.

Not because you tell me.

I wait. I watch. I listen.

It's plain to see

Your plan against me.

Ha, ha, ha.

Got you!

Thought me a fool?

Ha, ha, ha.

Liar or lover?

Sweat … It's okay.

Breathing changes with

unspoken words.

Smiling face

and telling eyes,

I watch … I listen.

Much is told.

Your legs, your arms

Tell me more as you squirm.

The silence is so loud.

No need to yell.

<u>Running heart</u>

Caught by surprise,

unknown to me.

When my running heart

ran from me.

Searched near … searched far.

Suddenly,

unknown to me,

my heart would find me.

<u>The reasons for war.</u>

Features: Beauty or Hideous

Knowledge: Genius or Dunce

Wealth: Rich or Poverty

Beginning characteristics of all things,

Understanding this is understanding self and others

—PEACE—

Yesterday

Yesterday, I held a friend.

Last painful breath he took.

He died no fault of mine.

I ask myself.

Could I have done more?

Tomorrow comes and it will be yesterday again.

George Prairie

Friends always,

Miss you, brother!

USMC

<u>Memories of a friend</u>

Hurtful memories of a lost friend, and

Yet I refuse to forget.

My heavy, pumping, painful heart

Will not forget.

Life's Final moment

"Be back!" were our words.

Time is swift.

Time is short.

Make it count.

Destinies change

in a single beat

or no beat at all.

Sudden final moment comes.

What? Why me?

No beginning!

No end!

Time is swift. Time is short …

<u>Endless</u>

Awaken in an ocean of endless dreams

Then one day awaken in endless sleep.

Within

Awake and in dreams you are within.

<u>Nightmare</u>

Maybe glimpse heart's desire?

Searching! So evasive.

Yell, only silence.

Legs ... so heavy

Nearby ... always farther.

Fear, sadness, anger grip you!

Then you awaken!

<u>Fooled</u>

A fool who makes a person

think he's a fool

is wise.

The person who thinks a fool to be a fool

is a fool.

A fool is not a fool

when he cannot be fooled.

Love answers

Pain, pain, so much pain!

Paralyzed,

Heartbeat slows,

Sweet death calls,

Heartbeat stops.

No life, no pain, only peace.

Still aware.

Distant painful calls for help,

Instant recognition coming back,

Painful gasp.

Spine pops, flooding pain, so much pain.

Love calls, love answers.

Hold on, babe! I'm coming!

<u>Mistakes</u>

Mistakes in the past

Never were my choice.

Forgotten years pass.

Recent remembered years

Asked for forgiveness.

Now I ask myself,

Should I forget or remember?

<u>Time</u>

Embracing lovers

embraced between heavenly blue

and earthly green.

Night's embrace awakens

with its moonly smile.

Stealthy time flees all embrace.

Lovers unaware of time's treachery

continue to embrace.

Time flees in fear to tell

if they will stay together.

Hearts as one can defy time.

Only time knows and in the end will tell.

Differences Version I

Both heaven's and grounded angels,

Weep and yell!

Saddened by our differences,

without our togetherness

the world will surely cease.

Differences Version II

Heaven's saddened Angels

Weep,

caused by our dividing,

worldly, seizing differences.

Only through unifying understanding

May we move heaven and earth.

<u>Eyes</u>

Eyes, eyes, eyes

Sleepy bedroom, knowing, teaching eyes.

No need to speak.

My eyes see what you're telling me.

Everlasting embrace

You're the earth under my protecting, everlasting, embracing
sky,

My wind caresses your mountains and valleys,

Listening to your whispering, breathing oceans.

Never alone, together as one, conquering cold perilous nights.

Strong will

Always remember:

A strong-willed person,

given enough time,

can surpass the accomplishments

of all the forgotten doubters that have ever existed.

<u>Insanity</u>

Helpless! No control.

Revenge!

Ponder.

No right! No wrong!

Why?

Doesn't matter now!

Consequences nonexistent,

Act!

Brief insanity or am I still …

Ah! Control!

Change

Forever changing

Oceans and mountains like emotions.

Love (peace) can become hate (war).

Hate (war) can become love (peace).

Acknowledge the sun;

become the sun.

Life

Like us,

Trees have

Fragile beginnings and ends,

Roots that give strength or weakness,

surrounded by

obstacles and feeding parasites,

till one day, we fall.

Thank you, Editor Victoria for your help. Everyone working at I universe thank you.

Thank you, Editor **George Nedeff, for this idea**. He suggested combining some of my poetry as one, or as vows. So I tried it. I liked this one. It can be read back and forth or together.

Combined from "Our love" and "Rain". Ill be combining more in the future.

<u>Our love</u>

Our love shall exist always,

      as tears from fallen lovers from the past, continue falling,

Tears wept and the breaths taken,

      In sadness or happiness,

Intermingled tears forever falling,

      from the sky.

Intermingled for all eternity.

      Meant to remind us not to fall.

Our love is and always will be. (This line couple reads together).

About the author

Angel Alexander StarWay has served in the U.S. Marine Corps as a radio operator, the navy as an aircraft electronics technician and a Seabee, and the Army National Guard as a mechanic on tanks and satellite/radio/phone systems. StarWay enjoys martial arts and extreme sports.

Born a Texan, StarWay has lived in Northern and Southern California, attended schools in California, Oklahoma, and Texas, and held jobs throughout the United States.

About the book

The poems reflect the author's thoughts on love, life, and death. Our world around us, seen through his eyes, gives us a moment or a lifetime of thought.